"PLEASE"

by Janet Riehecky
illustrated by Gwen Connelly

Created by

THE CHILD'S WORLD

Library of Congress Cataloging in Publication Data

Riehecky, Janet, 1953-
    Please / by Janet Riehecky ; illustrated by Gwen Connelly.
        p. cm. — (Manners matter)
    Summary: Describes various situations in which it is appropriate
to say, "Please."
    ISBN 0-89565-386-9
    1. Etiquette for children and youth.   [1. Etiquette.]
I. Connelly, Gwen, ill.   II. Title.   III. Series.
BJ1857.C5R5   1989
395'.122—dc19   88-16841
                                                              CIP
                                                              AC

2 3 4 5 6 7 8 9 10 11 12 R 97 96 95 94 93 92

"PLEASE"

MANNERS MATTER all day through.
Say, "I'm sorry" or "I didn't mean to."

"Please" or "May I?" or "After you"
Will help you with what you want to do.

When you treat others with respect and care,
You'll find you have friends everywhere.

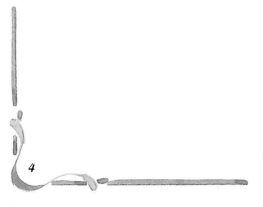

Say "Please" when you . . .

need some help . . .

want your dad to read you a
story . . .

need something you can't
reach . . .

want to try on your sister's
new necklace . . .

ask your mom to pass the
butter . . .

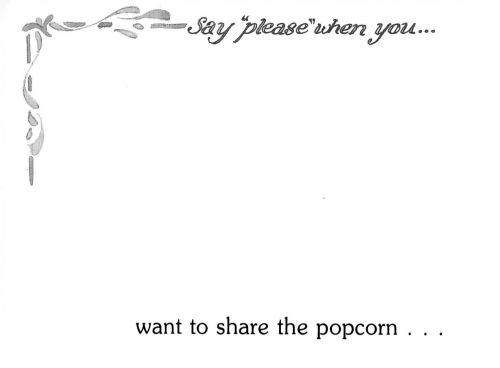

Say "please" when you...

want to share the popcorn . . .

ask your sister to finish drying
the dishes . . .

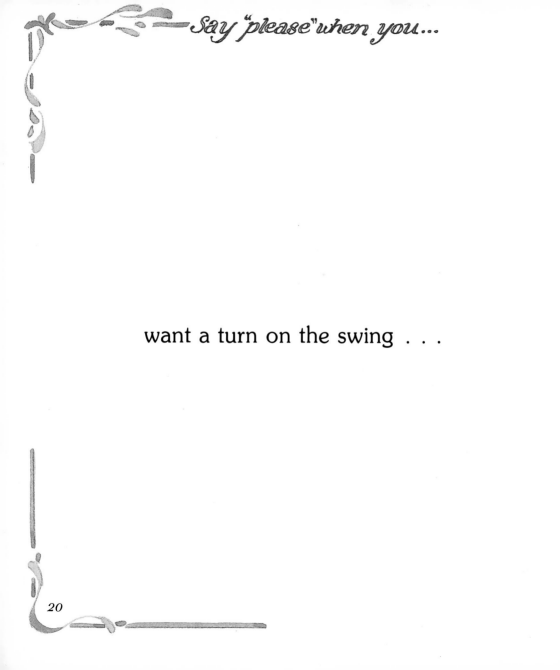

want a turn on the swing . . .

Say "please" when you...

want to go fishing with your
granddad . . .

want to join a jump-rope game . . .

want to change the TV program . . .

want a special doll . . .

want to stay up just a little longer.

Say "Please" whenever you
ask for anything.